MW00944144

CHEF BOY PRINCE TRAVELS
JAMAICA

Glenroy Brown and Marcus Cole

CHEF BOY PRINCE TRAVELS
JAMAICA

This book is dedicated to all the kids around the world, and to all of the aspiring chefs that find passion to pursue this incredible art. Throughout my career I have always loved working with children. I feel like it's important to share my knowledge and expertise of my craft anyway possible, writing this book was one of them. I have a platform and there is no greater privilege than to share that with the next generation.

-Glenroy Brown

This is for my Baby Bears a.k.a Chef Mina, if it weren't for you, this opportunity would have never presented itself. Thank you for allowing me to discover that I had one more trick up my sleeve! To Machiko and Mckenzie, thank you for your love and support and continuing to make me learn more about myself each and every day! For that, I am truly and forever grateful!

-Marcus Cole

Hello boys and girls!
My name is Chef Boy Prince, and it's a pleasure to meet you all. Together, we'll go on amazing adventures to some of the most beautiful countries around the world. We'll meet some of the most extraordinary Chefs each country has to offer and they'll show us how to prepare some of their country's most famous dishes. On our first adventure, we'll be traveling to Jamaica! So, grab your gear while I grab my knife bag, and let's get ready to go!

Jamaica is known for its beautiful weather, as well as its beaches. It's the third largest island in the Caribbean and famous for its rich culture, sports, Reggae music, and delicious foods.

Today, I'm very excited for you
to meet my good friend, Master Chef Glen.
I can't wait to take you on this awesome food journey.
Yea Mon!

"Hello, Master Chef Glen!
It's so nice to see you again!" exclaimed
Chef Boy Prince
"Good morning, Chef Boy Prince!" he
replied excitedly.

"I'm so happy to be here and I can't wait to explore this beautiful island and make some amazing dishes with you!" said Chef Boy Prince
With a big smile, Chef Glen asked, "Are you ready to head to the Coronation market down in Kingston?"
"Yes! I'm ready!" Chef Boy Prince answered.

8

(Stretching his arms out wide to show how big Coronation Market was): Chef Glen told Chef Boy Prince "It's the largest market in the English-speaking Caribbean. Here, we'll find a variety of foods and spices that represent the people of Jamaica."

"We'll get the ingredients needed
to create one of our most famous dishes,"
said Chef Glen.

"As you know, we're known for our bold flavor and spice. So, I decided we could make one of the island's favorites: jerk chicken," he said.

"Woo-hooooooo, YEAH MON!!!"
screamed Chef Boy Prince.

"What ingredients will we need to make jerk chicken?" asked Chef Boy Prince.
Eagerly Chef Glen replied, "We'll need chicken, ginger, allspice, garlic, scotch bonnet peppers, scallions, and thyme."
"Yuuuummmmmy, that sounds delicious!" declared Chef Boy Prince.

"And I know just the place to get them!" Chef Glen said, pointing to one particular shop. "We'll go to my favorite seller here in Coronation Market"

"Hello, Miss Femi. This is my friend,
Chef Boy Prince. He's come to Jamaica
to prepare jerk chicken with me."
"Excellent, you two have come
to the right place. I'm so glad to meet you!"
Miss Femi said.

After buying ingredients, Chef Glen tells Chef Boy Prince, "Once a year, I hold a small cooking class for the kids in the neighborhood. I told them you were coming and they're very excited."
With a big smile, Chef Boy Prince said, "That's incredible. I cannot wait to meet them all."

Back at the kitchen Chef Boy Prince notices Master Chef Glen's fancy knives. This reminds him of his knives inside his knife bag. As the kids come into the kitchen, they excitedly wait for Master Chef Glen to tell them what dish they'll be making today.

"Does anyone want to guess the delicious dish we'll make today?" he asked The kids responded gleefully; "Oxtails!" screamed one little boy.
"Curry chicken and goat!" exclaimed another.
"No, no, no. Ackee and saltfish!" a little girl shouted.

Impressed that the kids know so much about the different dishes, Chef Boy Prince was still surprised no one mentioned jerk chicken.

"All good guesses," said Chef Glen, "but today we're actually going to make (drumroll) ... classic jerk chicken," he revealed.

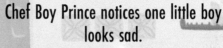

Chef Boy Prince notices one little boy looks sad.
"Hi, what's your name?" he asked.
"Lloyd." the little boy replied.

"Are you not excited about jerk chicken, Lloyd?"
"No, I'm not. I don't like spicy food because it makes my mouth burn. And if my friends see me, they might laugh at me." Lloyd said nervously.
"Don't worry, Lloyd. It'll be okay. We can easily leave the spicy ingredients out so that it's mild and not spicy. That's what cooking is all about," comforted Chef Boy Prince.

"Really? You can change a recipe?" Lloyd asked skeptical
"Absolutely!" exclaimed Chef Boy Prince. "Cooking is abo
having fun and being creative with the ingredients you ha
Changing a recipe to your liking is totally acceptable."

22

Chef Boy Prince and Lloyd rejoin the group as Master Chef Glen is telling the kids about the importance of personal hygiene, sanitation, and the safety rules of the kitchen.

"What is sanitation and safety and why is it important?" asked one little girl named Amelia.

"Sanitation is the process of handling food in ways that are clean and healthy. Chef Glen answered. "Safety means being careful in the kitchen to prevent an accident from happening, wearing clean aprons, slip resistant shoes, and properly bandaging any cuts at all times."

Chef Glen asked Chef Boy Prince to bring the chicken they would use for the jerk chicken recipe?"
Delighted to help, Chef Boy Prince said, "My pleasure."
As the children inch closer to watch and listen, Chef Boy Prince tells them that traditional jerk recipes are usually a two-day process, so they would begin today and finish the dish tomorrow.

Chef Glen began to detail the process, "The first part is for us to brine the chicken overnight." "What's a brine?" asked Lloyd.
"A brine is a mix of water, salt, and ingredients used for flavoring. It'll help the food last longer," Chef Glen explained. "Brining helps makes the chicken juicier."
After mixing up the brine and adding chicken to it, Chef Boy Prince puts everything in the refrigerator.
Master Chef Glen reminds the children to be at the kitchen the same time tomorrow!

When the children arrived the next day, they couldn't wait to finish the dish.
"Welcome back children!" shouted Chef Glen.
Chef Boy Prince pulls the chicken and brine out of the refrigerator and the delicious smell tickles all the kids' noses. Master Chef Glen begins to prepare the secret jerk sauce paste.

"Is jerk only for chicken?" asked on child.
"h no, jerk can be used for lots of different meat, including pork, fish, and beef." Chef Glen responded.
After giving a brief history of jerk, Chef Boy Prince finished the jerk paste. "Here it is, all finished!"
With a big smile on his face because of how good the chicken and paste look, Chef Boy Prince directs the children outside. "Now it's time to prepare the grill while the chicken marinates a little longer."

27

"That's one of my favorite sounds!" stated Chef Boy Prince, talking abo
the sizzle of the chicken being put on the grill.
One kid asked, "But what if we don't have an outdoor grill?"
"No problem, we have a griddle for that!" said Chef Glen.
After ten minutes, Master Chef Glen opens the grill, flips the
chicken over, then closes the lid. He says he will let the chicken cook o
this side for another ten minutes.

"Now kids, we're going to use a technique called basting. When we
baste, we brush juices, or in our case, jerk paste over the meat while
it's cooking to keep it moist and tender."
Chef Glen also explains another grilling technique to the kids.

"When grilling, sometimes you need less heat, so you can use less wood chips on one side so things cook slower." Chef Glen says. He then moves the chicken from the direct heat side to the lower heat side. After fifteen minutes, he removes the chicken from the grill and places it on a platter. But he is not done as he tells the kids, "There's one more important step we must do and that's to let the chicken rest."

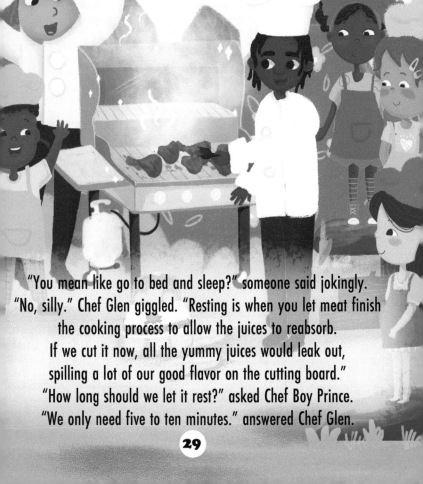

"You mean like go to bed and sleep?" someone said jokingly.
"No, silly." Chef Glen giggled. "Resting is when you let meat finish the cooking process to allow the juices to reabsorb.
If we cut it now, all the yummy juices would leak out, spilling a lot of our good flavor on the cutting board."
"How long should we let it rest?" asked Chef Boy Prince.
"We only need five to ten minutes." answered Chef Glen.

After waiting patiently for the jerk chicken to rest, the kids are ready to dig in.

"Let's eat!" shouted Chef Glen.

Master Chef Glen puts the jerk chicken on a platter and adds the BBQ sauce in a separate bowl. He also neatly arranges some white bread on the platter with the chicken. As the kids devour the delicious jerk chicken they made, Master Chef Glen and Chef Boy Prince talk to them about the importance of teamwork and how things are easier when people work together."

"So, how was the jerk chicken?" asked Master Chef Glen

The kids all agreed it was super delicious and the best jerk chicken they've ever ha

Master Chef Glen thanks the kids for attending the class and thanks Chef Boy Prince for making the trip to Jamaica to help make this classic dish.

"Thank you, Chef Boy Prince!" the kids shouted in unison. Chef Boy Prince feels joy that the kids are happy and is thankful the class wasn't just about cooking.
It's important that the children take back lessons they can use in everyday life. Even though things can be hard and challenging, believing in yourself is one of the most important things anyone can do.
"You are welcome! And now it's back to my travels!" said Chef Boy Prince.
"Where are you going next?" they asked.
"I'm off to Japan, the land of the rising sun!"

Recipe to be made with parent

Master Chef Glen's Perfect Jerk Chicken Recipe
(6-8 servings)

Chicken:

2 Breasts

2 Legs

2 Thighs

2 Wings

For the Brine:

½ cup kosher salt

¼ cup granulated sugar

1 tablespoon whole allspice

5 garlic cloves, crushed

1 jalapeño or Scotch bonnet pepper, halved

1-gallon cold water

Combine the salt, sugar, allspice, garlic, jalapeño or scotch bonnet pepper, ginger, and water in a large pan. Mix until the salt and sugar have dissolved. Add the chicken and cover with foil. Refrigerate overnight.

For the Jerk Paste:

1 cup soy sauce

½ cup fresh thyme leaves

½ cup Worcestershire sauce

1 tablespoon ground allspice

1 tablespoon light brown sugar

1 teaspoon kosher salt

1 teaspoon ground cinnamon

½ teaspoon ground cloves

4 garlic cloves, roughly chopped

3 bay leaves

2 bunches scallions, roughly chopped

2 Scotch bonnet peppers or jalapeño, halved

1-piece ginger, peeled and roughly chopped

Place all the ingredients in a blender or food processor and purée until smooth.

Directions:

1. After the chicken has been brined for 24 hours, remove from the brine and pat dry. Place in a shallow dish or pan and coat in 1 cup of the jerk paste. Cover directly with cling film or foil. Let it marinate for at least 60 minutes before grilling.

2. Soak wood chips in water for at least 30 minutes prior to grilling.

3. To grill the chicken: light grill (keep in mind you want to have one side on high/hot heat and the other side on low heat).

4. Add soaked wood chips over the coals.

5. Place the chicken on the hot/high heat side until charred on each side flipping once, about 8-10 minutes before your first flip.

6. Transfer chicken to the low heat side of the grill and cover in order to trap the smoke, flipping every 10-12 minutes (for about 40 minutes).

7. Using a kitchen thermometer, insert into the thickest part of the chicken. Thermometer should read 165°F.

8. Brush the chicken with some of the leftover jerk paste and cook until a little more charred (about 5 minutes).

9. Transfer chicken to a cutting board and let rest for 10 minutes.

10. Chop each piece in half. Serve with hot sauce or BBQ sauce on the side and with white bread.

CPSIA information can be obtained
at www.ICGtesting.com
Printed in the USA
BVHW020829131021
618835BV00007B/445